Practical
Meat Dishes

p^3

This is a P³ Book
This edition published in 2003

P³
Queen Street House
4 Queen Street
Bath BA1 1HE, UK

ISBN: 1-40542-387-0

Manufacture in China

NOTE

Cup measurements in this book are for American cups.
This book also uses imperial and metric measurements. Follow the same units
of measurement throughout; do not mix imperial and metric.
All spoon measurements are level: teaspoons are assumed to be 5 ml, and
tablespoons are assumed to be 15 ml. Unless otherwise stated,
milk is assumed to be whole milk, eggs and individual vegetables such as potatoes
are medium, and pepper is freshly ground black pepper.

The nutritional information provided for each recipe is per serving or per person.
Optional ingredients, variations, or serving suggestions have
not been included in the calculations. The times given for each recipe are an approximate
guide only because the preparation times may differ according to the techniques used by
different people and the cooking times may vary as a result of the type of oven used.

Recipes using raw or very lightly cooked eggs should be
avoided by infants, the elderly, pregnant women, convalescents,
and anyone suffering from an illness.

Contents

Introduction

Meat is very nutritious as well as delicious. It is a rich source of first-class protein, and provides a good supply of B vitamins, iron, and other trace elements. In prehistoric times, humans went out to hunt animals as a means of survival—the meat provided food and the skin provided clothing. Nowadays we do not need to hunt animals to survive, and many of us eat less meat than our ancestors did. Yet there is no doubt that meat can make a stunning centerpiece on the dinner table, and its versatility can be very useful in a busy lifestyle. For the health-conscious among you, there are many lean cuts of meat available, and the wide range of cooking techniques available nowadays, such as stir-frying, ensure that a little meat can go a long way.

Cuts of meat

Meat is available both home grown and imported. Some meats, such as New Zealand lamb, arrive frozen. Butchers cut their carcasses according to area and social and

economic requirements. For example, some religions have very specific guidelines and these dictate how an animal is slaughtered and cut. Likewise, butchers in deprived areas will not stock a lot of the expensive cuts—they will concentrate on the cheaper cuts, which are just as nutritious but normally need longer, slower cooking than their more expensive counterparts.

Storing meat

Place meat in the refrigerator as soon as possible after purchase. Take it out of its original wrapping and place on a plate large enough to contain any juices. Wrap it loosely in waxed paper or baking parchment and then, if desired, thin plastic wrap, but do let the air circulate freely around the meat by leaving the ends slightly free.

If you are buying frozen meat, place it in the freezer immediately. If you are buying fresh meat for the freezer, wrap it in heavy-duty freezer wrap, label clearly, and place it in the fast-freeze compartment.

There is absolutely no need to wash meat, but you can wipe it with clean, damp paper towels if you wish. Place

the meat in the coolest part of the refrigerator, ensuring that it is at the correct temperature of 38°F/4°C. Uncooked meat, such as joints and steaks, can be kept in these conditions for 3–4 days. However, raw ground meat, sausages, and offal should be eaten preferably on the day of purchase or within 1 day of purchase.

Cooked meats should be well wrapped to prevent the meat from drying out. If still hot, let cool first before thoroughly wrapping and placing in the refrigerator. Most cooked meats should be consumed, if home cooked, within 2–3 days. If you are reheating cooked meat, reheat until the meat is piping hot and only reheat once. If you are using store-bought, prepacked, cooked meat, use by the "use by" date and, once opened, treat as home-cooked meat.

Choosing meat

Generally speaking, choose meat that has a small amount of fat around it or through it. The fat should be firm, free from blemishes, and a pale color. The meat should be finely grained, firm, slightly elastic, and a good color. Freshly cut beef is bright red because the pigment in the tissue has been affected by the oxygen in the air. However, after a few hours the beef starts to turn a darker color. The color of the fat will vary according to the animal. Lamb fat is often quite a deep yellow, beef is pale, almost white,

and so is pork. The time of the year and the feed will also determine the fat color.

Another useful guide is to know the source of each specific cut. The leanest and most tenderest cuts are from the hindquarters, and the tougher cuts are from the neck, forequarters, and legs. The tougher cuts have done the most work and therefore will require long, slow cooking in order to tenderize the fibers that have become hardened. Meat from young animals is really tender. In some cases, animals are injected with an enzyme that softens the muscle fibers—this speeds up the natural processes, which gradually break down the protein cell walls as the carcass ages. This is why the carcasses are usually hung, to let this process happen.

calories are composed of fat, and of these calories only half comprise saturated fat. The recommended portion of beef is 75 g/2¾ oz per day.

Lamb contains similar levels of protein as beef and pork. However, it contains almost twice as much fat. This applies to all cuts of lamb, even the leg, which is often thought by many to be as lean as beef. Again, as with beef, lamb is a good source of B vitamins and the minerals zinc and magnesium. However, it should be avoided by people who have a high cholesterol level. Lamb also has a high vitamin A content, which can be toxic in high doses, so it should be avoided by women at the start of pregnancy.

Pork has perhaps the highest range of the B vitamins and, contrary to common belief, it is a lean meat and contains only a little more fat than lean beef. Only the delicious crackling you get from roast pork is very, very high in fat. Pork is a good source of zinc, and also selenium, which is an antioxidant and helps prevent heart disease and some cancers.

Poultry has grown in popularity over recent years and one of the main reasons is that it is thought to be really low in fat. In fact this is not so unless the skin is removed, preferably before cooking. If you eat the meat with the skin, it will have a higher fat content than beef.

Skinless turkey has the lowest fat content of all meats. Chicken and turkey contain a good proportion of selenium and B vitamins, as well as trace elements such as phosphorus and potassium. Duck contains selenium and B vitamins, but is higher in fat than chicken and turkey.

Handling meat

When cooking with meat, ensure that your hands, cutting board, and implements are scrupulously clean. It is a good practice to keep one board exclusively for meat preparation, and keep raw and cooked meats separate to prevent cross-contamination. Keep the cutting board clean: wash it thoroughly either with very hot, soapy water or a mild bleach in order to kill off any bacteria. If in doubt, try looking for marble boards, which harbor fewer bacteria, or plastic ones that have been impregnated with antibacterial compounds.

When cooking expensive cuts of beef and lamb, it is fine if the meat is cooked so that it is still slightly pink. However, ground meat and the cheaper cuts should be cooked so that the meat is thoroughly cooked and no pink remains. Pork should also be thoroughly cooked, as should all cuts of chicken and turkey.

Nutrition

Beef is an excellent source of protein and B vitamins, plus zinc and iron. The leaner cuts are not especially high in calories, with 100 g/3½ oz of lean roast beef containing only 175 calories. Just over one fourth of the

KEY	
	Simplicity level 1–3 (1 easiest, 3 slightly harder)
	Preparation time
	Cooking time

Chicken Soup with Stars

How delicious a simple, fresh soup can be. Chicken wings are good to use for making bouillon because the meat is very sweet and doesn't dry out.

NUTRITIONAL INFORMATION

Calories 119	Sugars 2g	
Protein 14g	Fat 2g	
Carbohydrate . . . 13g	Saturates 0g	

  20 mins   2¾ hrs

SERVES 5–6

I N G R E D I E N T S

¾ cup small pasta stars, or other very small pasta shapes

fresh parsley, chopped

C H I C K E N   B O U I L L O N

2 lb 12 oz/1.25 kg chicken pieces, such as wings or legs

10½ cups water

1 celery stalk, sliced

1 large carrot, sliced

1 onion, sliced

1 leek, sliced

2 garlic cloves, crushed

8 peppercorns

4 allspice berries

3–4 parsley stems

2–3 sprigs of fresh thyme

1 bay leaf

salt and pepper

2 Remove the chicken from the bouillon and set aside to cool. Continue simmering the bouillon, uncovered, for about 30 minutes. When the chicken is cool enough to handle, remove the meat from the bones and, if necessary, cut into bite-size pieces.

3 Strain the bouillon and remove as much fat as possible. Discard the vegetables and flavorings. (There should be about 7½ cups chicken bouillon.)

4 Bring the bouillon to a boil in a clean pan. Add the pasta and lower the heat so that the bouillon boils very gently. Cook for about 10 minutes, or until the pasta is tender but still firm to the bite.

5 Stir in the chicken meat. Taste the soup and adjust the seasoning if necessary. Ladle into warmed bowls and serve sprinkled with chopped parsley.

1 To make the bouillon, put the chicken in a large, flameproof casserole with the water, celery, carrot, onion, leek, garlic, peppercorns, allspice, herbs, and ½ teaspoon salt. Bring just to a boil; skim off the foam that rises to the surface. Lower the heat, partially cover, and simmer for 2 hours.

 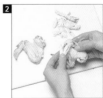 

Asian Duck Broth

This soup combines delicate flavors with a satisfying meaty taste.
Although duck is notoriously fatty, the legs are leaner than the breast.

NUTRITIONAL INFORMATION

Calories 98	Sugars 4g	
Protein 9g	Fat 3g	
Carbohydrate 9g	Saturates 1g	

🧊 10 mins   🕐 1¾ hrs

SERVES 4–6

INGREDIENTS

2 duck leg quarters, skinned

4 cups water

2½ cups chicken bouillon

1-inch/2.5-cm piece of fresh gingerroot, sliced

1 large carrot, sliced

1 onion, sliced

1 leek, sliced

3 garlic cloves, crushed

1 tsp black peppercorns

2 tbsp soy sauce

1 small carrot, cut into thin strips or slivers

1 small leek, cut into thin strips or slivers

1½ cups thinly sliced shiitake mushrooms

1 oz/25 g watercress or spinach leaves

salt and pepper

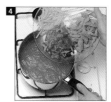

1 Put the duck in a large pan with the water. Bring just to a boil and skim off the foam that rises to the surface. Add the bouillon, ginger, carrot, onion, leek, garlic, peppercorns, and soy sauce. Reduce the heat, partially cover, and simmer gently for 1½ hours.

2 Remove the duck from the bouillon and set aside. When the duck is cool enough to handle, remove the meat from the bones, and slice thinly or shred into bite-size pieces, discarding any fat.

3 Strain the bouillon and press with the back of a spoon to extract all the liquid. Remove as much fat as possible. Discard the vegetables and flavorings.

4 Bring the bouillon just to a boil in a clean pan and add the strips of carrot and leek, and the mushrooms with the duck meat. Lower the heat and simmer gently for 5 minutes, or until the carrot is just tender.

5 Stir in the watercress or spinach leaves and continue simmering for 1–2 minutes, until they are wilted. Taste the soup and adjust the seasoning if necessary, adding a little more soy sauce if desired. Ladle the soup into warmed soup bowls and then serve immediately.

Split Pea & Ham Soup

A heartwarming soup, this is perfect for weekend lunches—or make it ahead for a nourishing midweek supper, all ready to reheat.

NUTRITIONAL INFORMATION

Calories 300   Sugars 5g
Protein . . . . .23g   Fat 9g
Carbohydrate . . .35g   Saturates 2g

 10 mins   1¼ hrs–1½ hrs

SERVES 6–8

I N G R E D I E N T S

2¼ cups field green peas

1 tbsp olive oil

1 large onion, finely chopped

1 large carrot, finely chopped

1 celery stalk, finely chopped

4 cups chicken bouillon or vegetable bouillon

4 cups water

8 oz/225 g lean smoked ham, finely diced

¼ tsp dried thyme

¼ tsp dried marjoram

1 bay leaf

salt and pepper

1 Rinse the peas under cold running water. Put them in a pan and cover generously with water. Bring to a boil and boil for 3 minutes, skimming off the foam from the surface. Drain the peas.

2 Heat the oil in a large pan over medium heat. Add the onion and cook, stirring occasionally, for about 3–4 minutes, until just softened.

3 Add the carrot and celery and continue cooking for 2 minutes. Add

the peas, pour in the bouillon and water, and stir to combine.

4 Bring just to a boil and add the ham to the soup. Add the thyme, marjoram, and bay leaf. Lower the heat, cover, and cook gently for 1–1½ hours, until the ingredients are very soft. Remove and discard the bay leaf.

5 Taste and adjust the seasoning if necessary. Ladle into warm soup bowls and serve immediately.

VARIATION

You could add sliced, cooked sausages instead of or in addition to the ham.

Beef Noodle Soup

Thin strips of beef are marinated in soy sauce and garlic to form the basis of this delicious soup. Served with noodles, it is both filling and delicious.

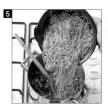

NUTRITIONAL INFORMATION

Calories	186	Sugars	.........1g
Protein	........17g	Fat	...........5g
Carbohydrate	...20g	Saturates	.......1g

35 mins

20 mins

SERVES 4

I N G R E D I E N T S

8 oz/225 g lean beef

1 garlic clove, crushed

2 scallions, chopped

3 tbsp soy sauce

1 tsp sesame oil

8 oz/225 g egg noodles

3½ cups beef bouillon

3 baby corn cobs, sliced

½ leek, shredded

4½ oz/125 g broccoli, cut into florets

pinch of chili powder

1 Using a sharp knife, cut the beef into thin strips and place in a large bowl with the garlic, scallions, soy sauce, and sesame oil.

2 Combine the ingredients in the bowl, turning the beef to coat. Cover and set aside to marinate in the refrigerator for 30 minutes.

3 Cook the noodles in a pan of boiling water for 3–4 minutes. Drain well and then set aside.

4 Put the beef bouillon in a large pan and bring to a boil. Add the beef, with the marinade, the baby corn cobs, shredded leek, and broccoli florets. Cover and simmer over low heat for 7–10 minutes, or until the beef and vegetables are tender and cooked through.

5 Add the noodles and chili powder and cook for another 2–3 minutes.

6 Transfer the soup to warmed bowls and serve immediately.

VARIATION
Vary the vegetables used or use those at hand. If preferred, use a few drops of chili sauce instead of chili powder, but remember it is very hot!

Chicken & Spinach Salad

Slices of lean chicken with young spinach leaves and a few fresh raspberries are served with a refreshing yogurt and honey dressing.

NUTRITIONAL INFORMATION

Calories ....235 Sugars 9g
Protein ....37g Fat 6g
Carbohydrate ....9g Saturates 2g

🍲 3½ hrs   🕐 25 mins

SERVES 4

I N G R E D I E N T S

4 boneless, skinless chicken breasts,
   5½ oz/150 g each

2 cups chicken bouillon

1 bay leaf

8 oz/225 g fresh young spinach leaves

1 small red onion, shredded

¾ cup fresh raspberries

salt and freshly ground pink peppercorns

freshly toasted croûtons, to garnish

D R E S S I N G

4 tbsp lowfat plain yogurt

1 tbsp raspberry vinegar

2 tsp honey

 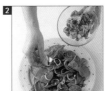 

1 Place the chicken breasts in a skillet. Pour over the bouillon and add the bay leaf. Bring to a boil, cover, and simmer for 15–20 minutes, turning halfway through, until the chicken is cooked through. Let cool in the liquid.

2 Arrange the spinach on 4 serving plates and top with the onion. Cover and chill.

3 Drain the cooked chicken and pat dry on absorbent paper towels. Slice the chicken breasts thinly and arrange, fanned out, on top of the spinach and onion. Sprinkle the salad with the raspberries.

4 To make the dressing, mix all the ingredients together in a small bowl. Drizzle a spoonful of dressing over each chicken breast and season with salt and ground pink peppercorns to taste. Serve the salad with freshly toasted croûtons.

VARIATION

This recipe is delicious with smoked chicken, but it will be more expensive and richer, so use slightly less. It would make an impressive appetizer for a dinner party.

Figs & Prosciutto

This colorful fresh salad is delicious at any time of the year.
Prosciutto di Parma is thought to be the best ham in the world.

NUTRITIONAL INFORMATION

Calories 121   Sugars 6g
Protein . . . . .1g   Fat 11g
Carbohydrate . . . .6g   Saturates 2g

 15 mins   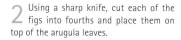 5 mins

SERVES 4

I N G R E D I E N T S

1½ oz/40 g arugula

4 fresh figs

4 slices prosciutto

4 tbsp olive oil

1 tbsp fresh orange juice

1 tbsp honey

1 small, fresh, red chile

1 Tear the arugula into manageable pieces and arrange on 4 individual serving plates.

2 Using a sharp knife, cut each of the figs into fourths and place them on top of the arugula leaves.

3 Using a sharp knife, cut the prosciutto into strips and scatter over the arugula and figs.

4 Place the oil, orange juice, and honey in a screw-top jar. Shake the jar vigorously, until the mixture emulsifies and forms a thick dressing. Transfer the dressing to a bowl.

5 Using a sharp knife, dice the chile. (You can remove the seeds first if you prefer a milder flavor.) Add the chopped chile to the dressing and mix well.

6 Drizzle the dressing over the prosciutto, arugula, and figs, tossing to mix well. Serve immediately.

COOK'S TIP
Chiles can burn the skin for several hours after chopping, so it is advisable to wear gloves when you are handling any very hot varieties and to wash your hands.

Rare Beef Pasta Salad

This mouthwatering salad is a meal in itself and would be perfect for an al fresco lunch, perhaps with a bottle of red wine.

NUTRITIONAL INFORMATION

Calories	575	Sugars	.........4g
Protein	........31g	Fat	..........33g
Carbohydrate	...44g	Saturates	.......9g

15 mins   30 mins

SERVES 4

INGREDIENTS

1 lb/450 g rump or sirloin steak in a single piece

4 cups dried fusilli

4 tbsp olive oil

2 tbsp lime juice

2 tbsp Thai fish sauce (see Cook's Tip)

2 tsp honey

4 scallions, sliced

1 cucumber, peeled and cut into 1-inch/ 2.5-cm chunks

3 tomatoes, cut into wedges

1 tbsp finely chopped fresh mint

salt and pepper

1 Season the steak with salt and pepper. Broil or pan-fry it for 4 minutes on each side. Let rest for 5 minutes, then slice thinly across the grain.

COOK'S TIP

Thai fish sauce, also known as *nam pla*, is made from salted anchovies and has quite a strong flavor, so it should be used with discretion. It is available from some supermarkets and from Asian food stores.

2 Meanwhile, bring a large pan of lightly salted water to a boil. Add the pasta, bring back to a boil, and cook for 8–10 minutes, or until tender but still firm to the bite. Drain the fusilli, refresh in cold water, and drain again thoroughly. Toss the fusilli in the olive oil and set aside until required.

3 Combine the lime juice, fish sauce, and honey in a small pan and cook over medium heat for 2 minutes.

4 Add the scallions, cucumber, tomatoes, and mint to the pan, then add the steak and mix together well. Season to taste with salt.

5 Transfer the fusilli to a large, warm serving dish and top with the steak and salad mixture. Serve just warm or let cool completely.

Hot & Sour Beef Salad

Thais are primarily fish-eaters, so beef usually appears on the menu only on feast days, but, as in this dish, a little can go a long way.

NUTRITIONAL INFORMATION

Calories 207	Sugars 7g	
Protein 15g	Fat 13g	
Carbohydrate 9g	Saturates 3g	

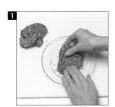

🕐 40 mins   🕐 8 mins

SERVES 4

I N G R E D I E N T S

1 tsp black peppercorns

1 tsp coriander seeds

1 dried, red bird-eye chile

¼ tsp Chinese five-spice powder

9 oz/250 g beef tenderloin

1 tbsp dark soy sauce

6 scallions

1 carrot

¼ cucumber

8 radishes

1 red onion

¼ head napa cabbage

2 tbsp peanut oil

1 garlic clove, crushed

1 tsp finely chopped lemongrass

1 tbsp chopped fresh mint

1 tbsp chopped fresh cilantro

D R E S S I N G

3 tbsp lime juice

1 tbsp light soy sauce

2 tsp soft, light brown sugar

1 tsp sesame oil

1 Crush the peppercorns, coriander seeds, and chile in a mortar with a pestle, then mix with the five-spice powder and sprinkle on a plate. Brush the beef all over with soy sauce, then roll it in the spices to coat evenly.

2 Cut the scallions into 2½-inch/ 6-cm lengths, then shred finely lengthwise. Place in ice water, until curled. Drain well.

3 Trim the carrot and cut into very thin diagonal slices. Halve the cucumber, scoop out and discard the seeds, then slice the flesh thinly. Trim the radishes and cut into flower shapes.

4 Slice the onion thinly. Roughly shred the napa cabbage leaves. Toss all the vegetables together in a large salad bowl.

5 Heat the oil in a skillet and cook the garlic and lemongrass, until golden. Add the beef and cook for 3–4 minutes, turning once. Remove from the heat.

6 Slice the beef thinly and toss into the salad with the mint and cilantro. Mix together the dressing ingredients and stir into the skillet, then spoon over the salad. Serve immediately.

Sherried Liver Brochettes

Economical and flavorsome, these tasty chicken liver skewers make an ideal light lunch or a perfect addition to a summer brunch party.

NUTRITIONAL INFORMATION

Calories 767	Sugars 3g	
Protein 31g	Fat 43g	
Carbohydrate ...51g	Saturates 8g	

3½–4½ hrs   15 mins

SERVES 6

I N G R E D I E N T S

14 oz/400 g chicken livers, trimmed
    and cleaned

3 strips rindless bacon

1 ciabatta loaf or small French stick

8 oz/225 g baby spinach

M A R I N A D E

⅔ cup dry sherry

4 tbsp olive oil

1 tsp wholegrain mustard

salt and pepper

M U S T A R D   M A Y O N N A I S E

1 tsp wholegrain mustard

8 tbsp mayonnaise

1 Cut the chicken livers into 2-inch/5-cm pieces. To make the marinade, combine the sherry, oil, mustard, and salt and pepper to taste in a shallow dish. Add the chicken livers to the marinade and toss until well coated. Set aside to marinate for 3–4 hours.

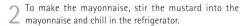

2 To make the mayonnaise, stir the mustard into the mayonnaise and chill in the refrigerator.

3 Stretch the bacon with the back of a knife and cut each strip in half. Remove the chicken livers from the marinade, reserving the marinade for basting. Wrap the bacon around half of the chicken liver pieces. Thread the bacon and chicken liver rolls and the plain chicken liver pieces alternately onto 6 presoaked wooden skewers.

4 Grill the skewers over hot coals for about 10–12 minutes, turning and basting with the reserved marinade frequently.

5 Meanwhile, cut the bread into 6 pieces and toast the cut sides on the barbecue grill, until golden brown.

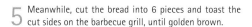

6 To serve, top the toasted bread with baby spinach and place the brochettes on top. Spoon over the mustard mayonnaise and serve immediately.

Murgh Pullau

In India, the meat and rice are cooked together for ease of preparation, but here they are cooked separately to ensure perfect timing.

NUTRITIONAL INFORMATION			
Calories	850	Sugars	........14g
Protein	.......44g	Fat	.........47g
Carbohydrate	...63g	Saturates	......20g

15 mins · 50 mins

SERVES 4–6

INGREDIENTS

1¾ cups basmati rice

4 tbsp ghee or butter

1 cup sliced almonds

¾ cup unsalted, shelled pistachios

4–6 skinless, boneless chicken breasts, each cut into 4 pieces

2 onions, thinly sliced

2 garlic cloves, finely chopped

2 bay leaves

1-inch/2.5-cm piece fresh gingerroot, chopped

6 green cardamom pods, lightly crushed

4–6 cloves

1 tsp ground coriander

½ tsp cayenne pepper

1 cup plain yogurt

½ cup boiling water

1 cup heavy cream

2–4 tbsp chopped fresh cilantro or mint

8 oz/225 g seedless green grapes, halved if large

salt and pepper

1 Bring a pan of salted water to a boil. Gradually pour in the rice, return to a boil, then simmer until the rice is just tender. Drain and rinse under cold running water. Set aside.

2 Meanwhile, heat the ghee in a deep skillet over medium heat. Add the nuts and cook, stirring constantly, for 3 minutes, until golden. Remove from the skillet and set aside.

3 Add the chicken to the skillet and cook for about 5 minutes, turning, until golden. Remove from the skillet. Add the onions to the pan. Cook for 10 minutes. Stir in the garlic, bay leaf, and spices and cook for 3 minutes.

4 Add 2–3 tablespoons of the yogurt and cook, stirring constantly, until all the moisture evaporates. Continue adding the remaining yogurt in the same way, until it is all incorporated.

5 Return the chicken and nuts to the skillet and stir to coat. Stir in ½ cup boiling water. Season with salt and pepper, cover, and cook over low heat for about 10 minutes, until the chicken is cooked through. Stir in the cream, cilantro, and grapes and remove the skillet from the heat.

6 Fork the rice into a bowl, then gently fold in the chicken and sauce. Let stand for 5 minutes before serving.

Drunken Noodles

Perhaps this would be more correctly named "drunkards' noodles,"
because it's a dish that is supposedly often eaten as a hangover cure.

NUTRITIONAL INFORMATION

Calories ....278 Sugars 3g
Protein ....12g Fat 7g
Carbohydrate ...40g Saturates 1g

20 mins   8–10 mins

SERVES 4

I N G R E D I E N T S

6 oz/175 g rice stick noodles

2 tbsp vegetable oil

1 garlic clove, crushed

2 small, fresh green chiles, chopped

1 small onion, thinly sliced

5½ oz/150 g lean ground pork or chicken

1 small, green bell pepper, seeded and
    finely chopped

4 kaffir lime leaves, finely shredded

1 tbsp dark soy sauce

1 tbsp light soy sauce

½ tsp sugar

1 tomato, cut into thin wedges

2 tbsp finely shredded fresh sweet basil
    leaves, to garnish

1 Soak the rice stick noodles in hot water for 15 minutes or according to the package directions. Drain well.

2 Heat the oil in a wok and stir-fry the garlic, chiles, and onion for 1 minute.

3 Stir in the pork or chicken and stir-fry over high heat for another minute, then add the bell pepper and continue stir-frying for another 2 minutes.

4 Stir in the lime leaves, soy sauces, and sugar. Add the noodles and tomato and toss well to heat thoroughly.

5 Sprinkle with the shredded basil leaves and serve hot.

COOK'S TIP

Fresh kaffir lime leaves freeze well,
so if you buy more than you need,
simply tie them in a tightly sealed
plastic freezer bag and freeze for
up to a month. They can be used
straight from the freezer.

Cheese & Ham Savory

Lean ham wrapped around crisp celery, topped with a light crust of cheese and scallions, makes a delicious light lunch.

NUTRITIONAL INFORMATION

Calories	188	Sugars	.........5g
Protein	........15g	Fat	..........12g
Carbohydrate	....5g	Saturates	......7g

🗇 10 mins   ⏱ 10 mins

SERVES 4

I N G R E D I E N T S

4 celery stalks, with leaves

12 thin slices of lean ham

bunch of scallions

¾ cup lowfat soft cheese with garlic and herbs

6 tbsp lowfat plain yogurt

4 tbsp freshly grated Parmesan cheese

celery salt and pepper

T O   S E R V E

tomato salad

crusty bread

1 Wash the celery. Remove the leaves and reserve for the garnish. Slice each stalk into 3 equal portions.

2 Cut any visible fat off the ham and lay the slices on a cutting board. Place a piece of celery on each piece of ham and roll up. Place 3 ham and celery rolls in each of 4 small, heatproof dishes.

3 Trim the scallions, then finely shred both the white and green parts. Sprinkle the scallions over the ham and celery rolls and season with celery salt and pepper.

4 Combine the soft cheese and yogurt and spoon the mixture over the ham and celery rolls.

5 Preheat the broiler to medium. Sprinkle 1 tablespoon grated Parmesan cheese over each portion and broil for about 6–7 minutes, until hot and the cheese has formed a crust. If the cheese starts to brown too quickly, lower the broiler setting slightly.

6 Garnish the ham and celery rolls with celery leaves and serve with a tomato salad and crusty bread.

COOK'S TIP

Parmesan is useful in lowfat recipes because its intense flavor means you need to use only a small amount.

Crispy Pork & Peanut Baskets

These tasty little appetite-teasers are an adaptation of a traditional recipe made with a light batter, but phyllo pastry is just as good.

NUTRITIONAL INFORMATION

Calories	243	Sugars	.........1g
Protein	........12g	Fat	..........16g
Carbohydrate	...12g	Saturates	.......3g

 10 mins   15 mins

SERVES 4

I N G R E D I E N T S

2 sheets phyllo pastry, each about 16½ x 11 inches/42 x 28 cm

2 tbsp vegetable oil

1 garlic clove, crushed

4½ oz/125 g ground pork

1 tsp Thai red curry paste

2 scallions, finely chopped

3 tbsp crunchy peanut butter

1 tbsp light soy sauce

1 tbsp chopped fresh cilantro

salt and pepper

sprigs of fresh cilantro, to garnish

1 Cut each sheet of phyllo pastry into 24 squares, 2¾ inches/7cm across, to make a total of 48 squares. Brush each square lightly with oil, and arrange the squares in stacks of 4 in 12 cups of a muffin pan, pointing outward. Press the phyllo stacks down into the muffin cups.

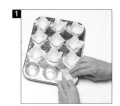

2 Bake the phyllo shells in a preheated oven, 400°F/200°C, for 6–8 minutes, until golden brown.

3 Meanwhile, heat the remaining oil in a wok. Add the garlic and stir-fry for 30 seconds, then stir in the pork and stir-fry over high heat for 4–5 minutes, until the meat is golden brown.

4 Add the curry paste and scallions and continue to stir-fry for another minute, then stir in the peanut butter, soy sauce, and chopped cilantro. Season to taste with salt and pepper.

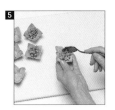

5 Spoon the pork mixture into the phyllo baskets and serve hot, garnished with cilantro sprigs.

COOK'S TIP

When using phyllo pastry, remember that it dries out very quickly and becomes brittle and difficult to handle. Work quickly and keep any sheets of phyllo you're not using covered with plastic wrap and a dampened cloth.

Lamb & Black Bean Burritos

Stir-fried marinated lamb strips are paired with earthy black beans in these tasty filled tortillas.

 4¼ hrs   15–20 mins

SERVES 4

INGREDIENTS

1 lb 7 oz/650 g lean lamb

3 garlic cloves, finely chopped

juice of ½ lime

½ tsp mild chili powder

½ tsp ground cumin

pinch of dried oregano

1–2 tbsp extra-virgin olive oil

14 oz/400 g cooked or canned black beans, seasoned with cumin, salt, and pepper

4 large flour tortillas

2–3 tbsp chopped fresh cilantro

salsa of your choice

salt and pepper

1 Slice the lamb into thin strips, then combine with the garlic, lime juice, chili powder, cumin, oregano, and olive oil. Season with salt and pepper. Set aside to marinate in the refrigerator for 4 hours.

2 Warm the black beans with a little water in a pan.

3 Heat the tortillas in an ungreased, nonstick skillet, sprinkling them with a few drops of water as they heat; wrap the tortillas in a clean dish towel as you work to keep them warm. Alternatively, heat through in a stack in the skillet, alternating the top and bottom tortillas so that they warm evenly.

4 Stir-fry the lamb in a heavy-bottomed, nonstick skillet over high heat, until browned on all sides. Remove from the heat.

5 Spoon some of the beans and browned meat into a tortilla, sprinkle with cilantro, top with salsa, and roll up. Repeat with the remaining tortillas and serve immediately.

VARIATION
Add a spoonful or two of cooked rice to each burrito.

Chicken with Purslane

Purslane has become fashionable, owing to its unique flavor and healthy dose of omega-3 fatty acids. It has always been popular in Mexico.

NUTRITIONAL INFORMATION

Calories	414	Sugars	. . . . .7g
Protein	. . . . .43g	Fat	. . . . .22g
Carbohydrate	. . . .11g	Saturates	. . . . . . .5g

1¾ hrs   50–60 mins

SERVES 4

INGREDIENTS

juice of 1 lime

6 garlic cloves, finely chopped

¼ tsp dried oregano

¼ tsp dried marjoram

¼ tsp dried thyme

½ tsp ground cumin

1 chicken, cut into 4 pieces

about 10 large, dried, mild chilies, such as pasilla, toasted

2 cups boiling water

2 cups chicken bouillon

3 tbsp extra-virgin olive oil

1 lb 9 oz/700 g tomatoes, charred under the broiler, skinned, and seeded

handful of corn tortilla chips, crushed

several large handfuls of fresh purslane, cut into bite-size lengths

½ lime

salt and pepper

lime wedges, to serve

 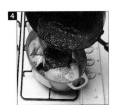

1 Combine the lime juice, half the garlic, the oregano, marjoram, thyme, cumin, and salt to taste. Rub the mixture over the chicken and set aside to marinate for at least an hour at room temperature or overnight in the refrigerator.

2 Place the chilies in a pan and pour the boiling water over them. Cover and set aside for 30 minutes, until softened. Remove the stems and seeds. Puree the chilies in a food processor or blender, adding just enough of the bouillon to make a smooth paste. Add the rest of the bouillon and mix well.

3 Heat 1 tablespoon of oil in a heavy skillet. Add the chili puree with the tomatoes and remaining garlic. Cook over medium heat, stirring, until it has thickened and reduced by about half.

4 Remove the chicken from the marinade, reserving any marinade juices. Brown the chicken in the remaining oil, then place in a flameproof casserole. Add any reserved juices and the reduced chili sauce. Cover and simmer over low heat for about 30 minutes, until the chicken is tender and cooked through.

5 Stir the crushed tortillas into the sauce and cook for a few minutes, then add the purslane. Season with salt, pepper, and a squeeze of lime juice. Heat through and serve with lime wedges.

Turkey with Cheese Pockets

Wrapping strips of bacon around the turkey helps to keep the cheese filling enclosed in the pocket—and adds extra flavor.

NUTRITIONAL INFORMATION

Calories 518	Sugars 0g	
Protein 66g	Fat 28g	
Carbohydrate 0g	Saturates 9g	

15 mins   20 mins

SERVES 4

INGREDIENTS

4 turkey breasts, about 8 oz/225 g each

4 portions fullfat cheese (such as Bel Paese), ½ oz/15 g each

4 sage leaves or ½ tsp dried sage

8 strips rindless bacon

4 tbsp olive oil

2 tbsp lemon juice

salt and pepper

TO SERVE

garlic bread

salad greens

cherry tomatoes

1 Carefully cut a pocket into the side of each turkey breast. Open out each pocket a little and season inside with salt and pepper to taste.

2 Place a portion of cheese into each pocket, spreading it a little with a knife. Tuck a sage leaf into each pocket or sprinkle with a little dried sage.

3 Stretch out the bacon with the back of a knife. Wrap 2 pieces of bacon around each turkey portion, so that the pocket openings are completely covered.

4 Combine the oil and lemon juice in a small bowl.

5 Grill the turkey over medium hot coals for about 10 minutes on each side, basting frequently with the oil and lemon mixture.

6 Place the garlic bread at the side of the barbecue grill and toast lightly.

7 Transfer the turkey to warm serving plates. Serve with the toasted garlic bread, salad greens, and cherry tomatoes.

VARIATION

You can vary the cheese you use to stuff the turkey—try grated mozzarella or slices of Brie or Camembert. Also try placing 1 teaspoon of red currant jelly or cranberry sauce into each pocket instead of the sage.

Duck with Lime & Kiwifruit

Tender breasts of duck served in thin slices, with a sweet, but very tangy lime and wine sauce, full of pieces of kiwifruit—sheer bliss.

NUTRITIONAL INFORMATION

Calories	264	Sugars	........20g
Protein	........20g	Fat	..........10g
Carbohydrate	...21g	Saturates	.......2g

🄖 🄖 🄖

🍧 1¼ hrs   ⏱ 15 mins

SERVES 4

I N G R E D I E N T S

4 boneless or part-boned duck breasts

grated rind and juice of 2 large limes

2 tbsp sunflower oil

4 scallions, thinly sliced diagonally

4½ oz/125 g carrots, cut into thin batons

6 tbsp dry white wine

¼ cup sugar

2 kiwifruit, peeled, halved, and sliced

salt and pepper

sprigs of fresh parsley and lime halves tied in knots (see Cook's Tip), to garnish

1 Trim any fat from the duck, then prick the skin all over with a fork and place in a shallow dish. Add half the grated lime rind and half the juice to the duck breasts, rubbing in thoroughly. Set aside in a cool place for at least 1 hour, turning the duck breasts at least once.

COOK'S TIP

To make the garnish, trim a piece off the bottom of each lime half so it stands upright. Pare off a thin strip of rind from the top of each lime half, about ¼ inch/5 mm thick, but do not detach it. Tie the strip into a knot with the end bending over the cut surface of the lime.

2 Drain the duck breasts, reserving the marinade. Heat 1 tbsp of oil in a wok. Add the duck and cook quickly to sear all over, then lower the heat, and continue to cook for about 5 minutes, turning several times, until just cooked through and well browned all over. Remove and keep warm.

3 Wipe the wok clean with paper towels and heat the remaining oil. Add the scallions and carrots and stir-fry for 1 minute, then add the remaining lime marinade, wine, and sugar. Bring to a boil and simmer for 2–3 minutes, until the mixture is slightly syrupy.

4 Add the duck breasts to the sauce, season to taste, and add the kiwifruit. Stir-fry for 1 minute, or until really hot and both the duck and kiwifruit are well coated in the sauce.

5 Cut each duck breast into slices, leaving a "hinge" at one end, open out into a fan shape, and arrange on plates. Spoon the sauce over the duck and sprinkle with the remaining pieces of lime rind. Garnish with parsley and knotted lime halves and serve immediately.

Honey-Glazed Duck

Chinese-style duck is incredibly easy to prepare, but makes an impressive and truly delicious entrée for a dinner party.

NUTRITIONAL INFORMATION

Calories 230   Sugars 9g
Protein . . . . .23g   Fat 9g
Carbohydrate . . .14g   Saturates 3g

 2¼ hrs   🕐 30 mins

SERVES 4

I N G R E D I E N T S

1 tsp dark soy sauce

2 tbsp honey

1 tsp garlic vinegar

2 garlic cloves, crushed

1 tsp ground star anise

2 tsp cornstarch

2 tsp water

2 large boneless duck breasts, about
    8 oz/225 g each

TO GARNISH

celery leaves

cucumber wedges

fresh chives

1 Combine the soy sauce, honey, garlic vinegar, garlic, and star anise. Blend the cornstarch with the water to form a smooth paste and stir it into the mixture.

2 Place the duck breasts in a shallow casserole. Brush with the soy marinade, turning them to coat completely. Cover and set aside to marinate in the refrigerator for at least 2 hours or overnight.

3 Remove the duck from the marinade and cook in a preheated oven, 425°F/220°C, for 20–25 minutes, basting frequently with the glaze.

4 Remove the duck from the oven and transfer to a preheated broiler. Broil for about 3–4 minutes to caramelize the top, without charring.

5 Remove the duck from the broiler pan and cut it into thin slices. Arrange the duck slices on a warmed serving dish, garnish with celery leaves, cucumber wedges, and fresh chives, and then serve immediately.

COOK'S TIP

If the duck begins to burn slightly while it is cooking in the oven, cover with foil. Check that the duck breasts are cooked through by inserting the point of a sharp knife into the thickest part of the flesh— the juices should run clear.

Maltese Rabbit with Fennel

Rabbit is a popular ingredient in Malta. In some restaurants it features as the house specialty, rather than seafood as one might expect.

NUTRITIONAL INFORMATION

Calories ....454 Sugars 3g
Protein ....36g Fat 23g
Carbohydrate ...19g Saturates 5g

🦀 🦀 🦀

15 mins   1¾ hrs

SERVES 4

I N G R E D I E N T S

5 tbsp olive oil

2 large fennel bulbs, sliced

2 carrots, diced

1 large garlic clove, crushed

1 tbsp fennel seeds

about 4 tbsp all-purpose flour

2 wild rabbits, cut into pieces

1 cup dry white wine

1 cup water

bouquet garni of 2 fresh flatleaf parsley
   sprigs, 1 fresh rosemary sprig, and 1 bay
   leaf, tied in a 3-inch/7.5-cm piece
   of celery

salt and pepper

thick crusty bread, to serve

T O   G A R N I S H

finely chopped fresh flatleaf parsley
   or cilantro

sprigs of fresh rosemary

1 Heat 3 tablespoons of the olive oil in a large, flameproof casserole over medium heat. Add the fennel and carrots and cook, stirring occasionally, for 5 minutes. Stir in the garlic and fennel seeds and cook for another 2 minutes, or until the fennel is tender. Remove the

fennel and carrots from the casserole with a slotted spoon and set aside.

2 Put the flour in a plastic bag and season with salt and pepper. Add 2 rabbit pieces and shake to coat lightly, then shake off any excess flour. Continue until all the pieces of rabbit are coated, adding more flour if necessary.

3 Add the remaining oil to the casserole. Cook the rabbit pieces for about 5 minutes on each side, until golden brown, working in batches. Remove the rabbit from the casserole as it is cooked.

4 Pour in the wine and bring to a boil, stirring to scrape up all the sediment from the bottom. Return the rabbit pieces, fennel, and carrots to the casserole and pour in the water. Add the bouquet garni and season with salt and pepper to taste.

5 Bring to a boil. Lower the heat, cover, and simmer for about 1¼ hours, until the rabbit is tender.

6 Remove and discard the bouquet garni. Garnish with parsley and rosemary and serve straight from the casserole with crusty bread to soak up the juices.

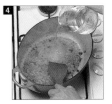

Meatballs in Red Wine Sauce

A different twist is given to this traditional and ever-popular pasta dish with a rich, but subtle, sauce.

45 mins   1½ hrs

SERVES 4

I N G R E D I E N T S

⅔ cup milk

2 cups fresh white bread crumbs

2 tbsp butter

generous ½ cup olive oil

3¼ cups sliced oyster mushrooms

2½ tbsp whole-wheat flour

scant 1 cup beef bouillon

⅔ cup red wine

4 tomatoes, skinned and chopped

1 tbsp tomato paste

1 tsp brown sugar

1 tbsp finely chopped fresh basil

12 shallots, chopped

1 lb/450 g ground steak

1 tsp paprika

1 lb/450 g dried egg tagliatelle

salt and pepper

sprigs of fresh basil, to garnish

1 Pour the milk into a bowl, add the bread crumbs, and set aside to soak for 30 minutes.

2 Heat half the butter and 4 tablespoons of the oil in a pan. Cook the mushrooms for 4 minutes, then stir in the flour and cook for 2 minutes. Add the bouillon and wine and simmer for 15 minutes. Add the tomatoes, tomato paste, sugar, and basil. Season and simmer for 30 minutes.

3 Mix the shallots, steak, and paprika with the bread crumbs and season to taste. Shape the mixture into 14 meatballs.

4 Heat 4 tablespoons of the remaining oil and the rest of the butter in a large skillet. Cook the meatballs, turning frequently, until brown all over. Transfer to a deep casserole, pour over the red wine and mushroom sauce, cover, and bake in a preheated oven, 350°F/180°C, for 30 minutes.

5 Bring a pan of lightly salted water to a boil. Add the pasta and remaining oil, bring back to a boil, and cook for 8–10 minutes, or until tender but still firm to the bite. Drain and transfer to a serving dish. Remove the casserole from the oven and cool for 3 minutes. Pour the meatballs and sauce onto the pasta, garnish with basil, and serve.

Red-Hot Beef with Cashews

Hot and spicy, these quick-cooked beef strips are very tempting.
Serve them with lots of plain rice and cucumber slices to offset the heat.

NUTRITIONAL INFORMATION

Calories ....257 Sugars 1g
Protein ....32g Fat 13g
Carbohydrate ....3g Saturates 4g

2¼–3¼ hrs   10 mins

SERVES 4

INGREDIENTS

1 lb 2 oz/500 g boneless, lean beef sirloin, thinly sliced

1 tsp vegetable oil

1 tsp sesame oil

4 tbsp unsalted cashews

1 scallion, thickly sliced diagonally

cucumber slices, to garnish

MARINADE

1 tbsp sesame seeds

1 garlic clove, chopped

1 tbsp finely chopped fresh gingerroot

1 fresh, red bird-eye chile, chopped

2 tbsp dark soy sauce

1 tsp red curry paste

1 Cut the beef into ½-inch/1-cm wide strips. Place the strips in a large, nonmetallic bowl.

2 To make the marinade, dry-cook the sesame seeds in a heavy pan over medium heat for 2–3 minutes.

3 Place the seeds in a mortar with the garlic, ginger, and chile and grind to a smooth paste with a pestle. Add the soy sauce and curry paste and mix well.

4 Spoon the paste over the beef strips and toss well to coat the meat evenly. Cover and set aside to marinate in the refrigerator for 2–3 hours or overnight.

5 Heat a heavy skillet or ridged grill pan until very hot, then brush with vegetable oil. Add the beef strips and cook quickly, turning frequently, until lightly browned. Remove from the heat and spoon into a pile on a warmed serving dish.

6 Heat the sesame oil in a small pan and cook the cashews, until golden. Add the scallion and stir-fry for 30 seconds. Sprinkle the mixture onto the beef and serve garnished with cucumber.

Sliced Beef with Yogurt

Roasting the spices for this dish gives it a nice dark color and a richer flavor. Serve with chapatis and white lentils for a substantial meal.

NUTRITIONAL INFORMATION		
Calories 981	Sugars 5g	
Protein 33g	Fat 94g	
Carbohydrate 6g	Saturates 14g	

🥄 20 mins   🕐 45 mins

SERVES 4

INGREDIENTS

1 lb/450 g lean beef slices, cut into 1-inch/2.5-cm slices

5 tbsp plain yogurt

1 tsp finely chopped fresh gingerroot

1 tsp crushed garlic

1 tsp chili powder

pinch of ground turmeric

2 tsp garam masala

1 tsp salt

2 cardamoms

1 tsp black cumin seeds

2 oz/55 g ground almonds

1 tbsp dry unsweetened coconut

1 tbsp poppy seeds

1 tbsp sesame seeds

1¼ cups vegetable oil

2 medium onions, finely chopped

1¼ cups water

2 fresh green chiles

a few fresh cilantro leaves, chopped

1 Place the beef in a large bowl. Combine with the yogurt, ginger, garlic, chili powder, turmeric, garam masala, salt, cardamoms, and black cumin seeds and set aside until required.

2 Dry-cook the ground almonds, coconut, poppy seeds, and sesame seeds in a heavy skillet until golden, shaking the pan occasionally.

3 Transfer the spice mixture to a food processor and process until finely ground. (Add 1 tablespoon water to blend, if necessary.) Add the ground spice mixture to the meat mixture and combine.

4 Heat a little oil in a large pan and cook the onions, until golden brown. Remove the onions from the pan. Stir-fry the meat in the remaining oil for about 5 minutes, then return the onions to the pan and stir-fry for another 5–7 minutes. Add the water, cover, and simmer over low heat, stirring occasionally, for about 25–30 minutes. Add the chiles and cilantro and serve hot.

Saucy Sausages

Although there is much more to barbecues than sausages, they can make a welcome appearance from time to time.

NUTRITIONAL INFORMATION

Calories	369	Sugars	........18g
Protein	........15g	Fat	..........24g
Carbohydrate	...25g	Saturates	.......7g

10 mins   35 mins

SERVES 4

I N G R E D I E N T S

2 tbsp sunflower oil

1 large onion, chopped

2 garlic cloves, chopped

8 oz/225 g canned chopped tomatoes

1 tbsp Worcestershire sauce

2 tbsp brown fruity sauce

2 tbsp molasses sugar

4 tbsp white wine vinegar

½ tsp mild chili powder

¼ tsp mustard powder

dash of Tabasco sauce

1 lb/450 g sausages

salt and pepper

bread finger rolls, to serve

COOK'S TIP

Choose any well-flavored sausages for this recipe. Bratwurst is a good choice, as are uncooked Kielbasa sausages. Venison sausages have a good, gamey flavor and taste marvelous cooked on the barbecue grill.

1 To make the sauce, heat the oil in a small pan and cook the onion and garlic for 4–5 minutes, until softened and just beginning to brown.

2 Add the tomatoes, Worcestershire sauce, brown fruity sauce, sugar, wine vinegar, chili powder, mustard powder, Tabasco sauce, and salt and pepper to taste. Bring to a boil.

3 Lower the heat and simmer gently for 10–15 minutes, until the sauce begins to thicken slightly. Stir occasionally so that the sauce does not burn and stick to the bottom of the pan. Set aside and keep warm, until required.

4 Grill the sausages over hot coals for 10–15 minutes, turning frequently. Do not prick them with a fork or the fat will run out and cause a fire.

5 Insert the sausages into the bread rolls and serve immediately with the barbecue sauce.

Pork Stir-Fry with Vegetables

This is a very simple dish, which lends itself to almost any combination of vegetables that you have at hand.

NUTRITIONAL INFORMATION

Calories 216   Sugars 3g
Protein . . . . .19g   Fat 12g
Carbohydrate . . . .5g   Saturates 3g

 5 mins   15 mins

SERVES 4

I N G R E D I E N T S

2 tbsp vegetable oil

2 garlic cloves, crushed

½-inch/1-cm piece of fresh gingerroot, cut into slivers

12 oz/350 g lean pork tenderloin, thinly sliced

1 carrot, cut into thin strips

1 red bell pepper, seeded and diced

1 fennel bulb, sliced

1 oz/25 g water chestnuts, halved

1½ cups bean sprouts

2 tbsp Chinese rice wine

1¼ cups pork bouillon or chicken bouillon

pinch of dark brown sugar

1 tsp cornstarch

2 tsp water

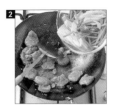

1 Heat the oil in a preheated wok. Add the garlic, ginger, and pork. Stir-fry for 1–2 minutes, until the meat is seared.

2 Add the carrot, bell pepper, fennel, and water chestnuts and stir-fry for about 2–3 minutes.

3 Add the bean sprouts and stir-fry for 1 minute. Remove the pork and vegetables, set aside, and keep warm.

4 Add the Chinese rice wine, pork bouillon or chicken bouillon, and sugar to the wok. Blend the cornstarch to a smooth paste with the water and stir it into the sauce. Bring to a boil, stirring constantly, until thickened and clear.

5 Return the meat and vegetables to the wok and cook for 1–2 minutes, until heated through and coated with the sauce. Serve immediately.

VARIATION
Use dry sherry instead of the Chinese rice wine if you have difficulty obtaining it.

Pot Roasted Leg of Lamb

This dish from the Abruzzi region of Italy uses a slow cooking method. The meat absorbs the flavorings and becomes very tender.

NUTRITIONAL INFORMATION

Calories 734   Sugars 6g
Protein . . . . .71g   Fat 42g
Carbohydrate . . . .7g   Saturates 15g

 35 mins   3 hrs

SERVES 4

I N G R E D I E N T S

3 lb 8 oz/1.6 kg leg of lamb

3–4 sprigs of fresh rosemary

4 oz/115 g bacon strips

4 tbsp olive oil

2–3 garlic cloves, crushed

2 onions, sliced

2 carrots, sliced

2 celery stalks, sliced

1¼ cups dry white wine

1 tbsp tomato paste

1¼ cups bouillon

12 oz/350 g tomatoes, skinned, seeded,
   and cut into fourths

1 tbsp chopped fresh parsley

1 tbsp chopped fresh oregano or marjoram

salt and pepper

sprigs of fresh rosemary, to garnish

1 Wipe the joint of lamb all over, trimming off any excess fat, then season with salt and pepper, rubbing in well. Lay the sprigs of rosemary over the lamb, cover evenly with the bacon strips, and tie in place with string.

2 Heat the oil in a skillet and cook the lamb for about 10 minutes, turning several times. Remove from the skillet.

3 Transfer the oil from the skillet to a large, flameproof casserole and cook the garlic and onions for 3–4 minutes, until beginning to soften. Add the carrots and celery and cook for a few minutes longer.

4 Lay the lamb on top of the vegetables and press down to partly submerge. Pour the wine over the lamb, add the tomato paste, and simmer for about 3–4 minutes. Add the bouillon, tomatoes, and herbs, and season to taste with salt and pepper. Bring back to a boil for another 3–4 minutes.

5 Cover the casserole tightly and cook in a moderate oven, 350°F/180°C, for 2–2½ hours, until very tender.

6 Remove the lamb from the casserole and, if preferred, take off the bacon and herbs along with the string. Keep warm. Strain the juices, skimming off any excess fat, and serve in a pitcher. The vegetables may be arranged around the pot roast or in a serving dish. Garnish with sprigs of fresh rosemary.

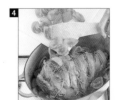

Lamb Cooked in Spinach

This succulent lamb dish shows the influence of southern Indian cooking and is both quick and easy to prepare.

NUTRITIONAL INFORMATION

Calories 944   Sugars 8g
Protein . . . . .31g   Fat 87g
Carbohydrate . . . .11g   Saturates 12g

 5 mins   1¼ hrs

SERVES 4

I N G R E D I E N T S

1¼ cups vegetable oil

2 medium onions, sliced

¼ bunch of fresh cilantro

3 fresh green chiles, chopped

1½ tsp finely chopped fresh gingerroot

1½ tsp crushed fresh garlic

1 tsp chili powder

½ tsp ground turmeric

1 lb/450 g lean lamb, with or
    without the bone

1 tsp salt

2 lb 4 oz/1 kg fresh spinach, trimmed,
    washed, and chopped, or 15 oz/
    425 g canned spinach

3 cups water

fresh red chiles, finely chopped, to garnish

4 Add the lamb and stir-fry for another
5 minutes. Add the salt and the fresh
or canned spinach and cook, stirring
occasionally, for another 3–5 minutes.

5 Stir in the water, cover, and cook over
low heat for about 45 minutes.
Remove the lid and check the meat. If it is
not tender, turn the meat over, increase
the heat, and cook, uncovered, until the
surplus water has been absorbed. Stir-fry
the mixture for another 5–7 minutes.

6 Transfer the lamb and spinach
mixture to a warmed serving dish and
garnish with finely chopped red chiles
and the remaining chopped green chile.
Serve immediately.

1 Heat the oil in a pan and cook the
onions until they turn pale gold.

2 Add the fresh cilantro and 2 of the
chopped green chiles to the pan and
stir-fry for 3–5 minutes.

3 Lower the heat and stir in the ginger,
garlic, chili powder, and turmeric.

Veal Chops with Salsa Verde

This vibrant, green Italian sauce adds a touch of Mediterranean flavor to any simply cooked meat or seafood.

NUTRITIONAL INFORMATION

Calories 481	Sugars 1g
Protein 41g	Fat 34g
Carbohydrate 2g	Saturates 5g

🍲 10 mins   🕐 5 mins

SERVES 4

I N G R E D I E N T S

4 veal chops, such as loin chops, about 8 oz/225 g each and ¾ inch/2 cm thick

garlic-flavored olive oil, for brushing

salt and pepper

fresh oregano or basil leaves, to garnish

S A L S A   V E R D E

2 cups fresh flatleaf parsley leaves

3 canned anchovy fillets in oil, drained

1½ tsp capers in brine, rinsed and drained

1 shallot, finely chopped

1 garlic clove, halved, green core removed, and chopped

1 tbsp lemon juice

6 large, fresh basil leaves or ¾ tsp freeze-dried basil

2 sprigs of fresh oregano or ½ tsp dried oregano

½ cup extra-virgin olive oil

1 To make the salsa verde, put the parsley, anchovies, capers, shallot, garlic, lemon juice, basil, and oregano in a blender or food processor and process until they are thoroughly chopped and blended.

2 With the motor running, add the oil through the top or feeder tube and process until thickened. Season with pepper to taste. Scrape into a bowl, cover with plastic wrap, and chill in the refrigerator.

3 Lightly brush the veal chops with olive oil and season to taste with salt and pepper. Place under a preheated broiler and cook for about 3 minutes. Turn over, brush with more oil, and broil for another 2 minutes, until cooked when tested with the tip of a knife.

4 Transfer the chops to warmed individual plates and spoon a little of the chilled salsa verde beside them. Garnish the chops with fresh oregano or basil and serve with the remaining salsa verde handed separately.

COOK'S TIP

The salsa verde will keep for up to 2 days in a covered container in the refrigerator. It is also marvelous served with broiled red snapper.